LEï

RECIPES

compiled by
Simon Haseltine

Illustrated with scenes
of cottage life

SALMON

Index

Cover pictures *front:* "Breakfast Time" *by Harry Brooker*
back: "First Birthday Party" *by Frederick Hardy*
Title page: "The Chimney Corner" *by Joseph Clark*

Printed and published by Dorrigo, Manchester, England © Copyright

Cold Meat and Leek Pie

Good for picnics and with salads.

1lb. selection of cold cooked meats (cubed) (chicken or turkey plus ham ideal)
¾ pint chicken or turkey stock (make from the leftover carcass)
4 leeks
Leftover peas, or broccoli or sweet corn (no more than half a cup)
8 oz. short crust pastry   1 oz. flour   Large knob of butter
1 egg   1 teaspoon mustard powder
Pinch of salt and ground black pepper

Melt the butter in a saucepan, stir in the flour and cook for a few minutes. Then slowly add the stock and gently bring to a boil, stirring all the time. Simmer until the stock has thickened, then add the mustard and seasoning.

Place the cubed cold meat, chopped leeks and vegetables into an ovenproof pie dish, season and pour over the sauce until just covered. Roll the pastry out and cover the pie, pressing down the edges. Make a small hole in the top, then brush with beaten egg. Bake in preheated oven at 400°F or Mark 6 for 30 to 40 minutes when the crust is cooked and golden in colour. Serves 6.

"Good News" by George Smith

Monday Stew

So called as commonly eaten every Monday,
using up all the leftover weekend meat and vegetables.

1 lb. cooked or raw meat (beef, chicken, turkey, pork – sliced or cubed)
2 lb. vegetables (selection from raw potatoes, courgettes, carrots,
swede, green beans, leeks etc left over from the weekend)
Beef stock (Sunday's gravy plus some additional water ideal)
Pearl barley (around half a cup)   2 tablespoons rolled oats
Large onion   Ground black pepper

Soak the pearl barley in some boiling water. If using raw meat, fry off in a little oil to brown. Prepare your selection of vegetables by peeling and cutting into small cubes or slices. Add these, together with the pearl barley to the meat and top with stock until all the meat and vegetables are just covered. Stir in the rolled oats, add black pepper to taste and cook in a slow cooker on a low heat for 6 hours. Serve with plenty of Champ (see recipe page 24). If there's any left, even better reheated to piping hot the following day. Serves 6.

Sausage Risotto

A wonderful way to use up leftover sausages.

**2 cooked sausages (sliced)   1 onion (chopped)
1 carrot (grated)   Tin chopped tomatoes
12 oz. cooked rice   Pinch mixed herbs
Tomato ketchup   Basil leaves
Oil**

Fry the onions and grated carrot until soft, then add the sausages and cook for a few more minutes. Add the rice and mix well before adding the tinned chopped tomatoes, tomato ketchup and herbs. Stir and simmer for 5 minutes.

To serve, pile into a dish and sprinkle with basil leaves. Serves 4.

Chilli

If there is mince left over from the previous day's meal try this tasty chilli.

12 oz. minced beef (use leftover mince from a previous day's meal)
1 onion (chopped)   4 button mushrooms (sliced)
½ teaspoon dried flaked chilli
1 stock cube   Pinch mixed herbs
1 tablespoon rolled oats
Tin chopped tomatoes (plus a little water)
Hot chilli sauce (to taste!)

Fry the onions in a little oil until soft, then add the minced beef, crumbled stock cube and herbs and fry until brown. Drain any excess fat, then return to the heat with the chopped tomatoes, mushrooms, flaked chilli and rolled oats. Simmer gently for around 20 minutes, adding a little more water, as required. Season to taste with your favourite chilli sauce, stir and cook a little longer. Serve with rice or a jacket potato. Variation – use a tin of baked beans instead of the tomatoes. Serves 2 to 3.

Ham Fritters

Delicious memories of Spam fritters.

3 oz. ham (chopped finely)   1 onion (chopped finely)
4 oz. flour   3 fl. oz. warm water
1 egg white   Pinch mixed herbs
1 lemon rind, grated   Seasoning
Oil for deep frying

Fry the chopped onion until lightly brown. Mix the flour and water to a smooth paste, add to the ham, onion, lemon rind, herbs and seasoning. Fold in the stiffly whisked egg white and form into small balls. Deep fry the fritters until golden brown and drain on kitchen paper. Serve with a salad and some hot English mustard. Serves 2.

"A Cosy Party" by Mary Kindon

Meat and Potato Pie

Uses up leftover meat, vegetables and gravy.

10 oz. cold meat (chicken, lamb or beef works well)
1 lb. parboiled potatoes (sliced)   1 onion (chopped)
4 oz. leftover vegetables (e.g. sprig broccoli, a few peas, cubed carrot/swede)
½ pint gravy   Pepper and salt

Line the bottom of a pie dish with half the slices of potato then cover with a layer of meat, onions and vegetables, finish with the remaining potato. Season with plenty of pepper and a little salt. Pour over the gravy and cover with baking paper.

Bake in preheated oven for 45 minutes at 400°F or Mark 6 – remove baking paper with 15 minutes to go to allow potatoes to brown.

Alternative – use slightly less potato and cover with a sheet of puff pastry and bake until golden brown. Serves 4.

Turkey Blanquette

A French twist to using up leftover turkey and vegetables.

1 lb. cold turkey (sliced)   12 oz. chicken stock
1 onion (chopped)
4 oz. cooked vegetables (sliced carrots, leeks, peas)
Knob butter   2 tablespoons flour
Pinch mixed herbs   4 tablespoons cream or milk
2 egg yolks   Seasoning

Heat the butter in a saucepan and fry the onion for a few minutes. Add the flour and stir before gradually mixing the stock. Add the herbs, then stir until boiling and then simmer for a further 10 minutes to reduce and thicken. Season to taste, then add the turkey and vegetables and heat through until piping hot.

Meanwhile, blend the cream or milk and egg together and add to the stew. Heat through for a further 5 minutes, stirring gently, then serve with rice. Serves 2.

"The Village School" by Alfred Rankley

Frizzled Beef

"Frizzled" – what a lovely term, found in an old recipe book.

4 oz. cold beef (sliced)
½ lb. cold potatoes (mashed)
1 onion (chopped)   Seasoning
Onion gravy   Oil for frying

Fry the slices of cooked beef until brown (frizzled), remove and keep warm. Then fry the onion until brown and fold into the mashed potato. Season to taste and form into cakes and fry for a further 5 minutes until brown on both sides. Arrange the potato cakes on a plate with the frizzled beef on top and serve with delicious onion gravy. Serves 2.

Roast Beef Puddings with Bubble and Squeak

Use up your Sunday roast leftovers with this tasty Monday teatime treat.

Small amount of cold beef (sliced) – 4 oz. ideal
4 oz. flour   1 egg   8 fl. oz. milk
Pinch mixed herbs   Pinch mustard powder   Oil

Make the batter by blending the egg and milk slowly into the flour, then add the herbs and mustard powder. Whisk well to form lots of air bubbles (the secret of any good Yorkshire pudding). Heat the oil in your Yorkshire pudding tins until smoky hot and carefully place the slices of cold beef into the hot oil and pour over the batter.

Cook in preheated hot oven at 450°F or Mark 8 for around 30 minutes or until risen and golden and serve with bubble and squeak and onion gravy. Serves 4. Alternative – add some fried onion if not enough beef.

Christmas Croquettes

Delicious also with leftover chicken at any time of the year.

1 lb. cooked turkey (chopped)   1 onion (chopped)
Large knob butter   2 tablespoons flour
7 fl. oz. milk   1 tablespoon cranberry sauce
1 lemon (juice)   Pinch mixed herbs
1 egg (beaten)   4 oz. breadcrumbs   Oil for frying
Seasoning

Fry the onion in the butter for a few minutes then add the flour and stir well before gradually adding the milk to form a thick sauce, cooking for 3 further minutes. Fold in the turkey, cranberry sauce, herbs and lemon juice and heat through for a few more minutes. Season to taste. Remove from heat, cool, then place in fridge until chilled. Form the cold mixture into croquettes, dip into the egg and cover with breadcrumbs, then fry until golden brown on all sides.

Chicken or Turkey Stir Fry

*A very quick and easy stir fry using leftover chicken
and a few tins from the store cupboard.*

8 oz. cooked chicken or turkey (sliced). If you have less, add sliced mushrooms.
1 onion (chopped)   1 tin Chinese vegetables (drained)
1 jar your favourite Chinese sauce
6 oz. rice

Cook the rice in accordance with the packet instructions. In the meantime, fry the onion and add the sliced chicken or turkey (or mushrooms) and drained Chinese vegetables. Add the sauce and heat through until piping hot. Drain the rice and serve with the Chinese chicken. Serves 2.

"Rustic Courtship" by William Midwood

Spicy Curry

Curries are ever popular and are ideal for using up leftover ingredients.

Meat curry:
Around 8 oz. leftover chicken or turkey or minced beef (chopped)
1 onion (sliced)   Mushrooms (allow 2 per person) (sliced)
1 can tin chopped tomatoes   1 oz. almonds (flaked)
1 heaped teaspoon, or more to taste, curry powder or paste
(Madras powder makes for a spicy meal)

Fry the onion until soft, add the mushrooms and curry powder or paste and fry for a few more minutes. Add the cooked meat and almonds and coat with the onion mixture. Add the tinned tomatoes (save some of the juice for the Bombay potatoes below) and simmer for 10 minutes.

Vegetable side dish:
1 cold cooked parsnip (sliced)   Olive oil   1 teaspoon Madras curry powder

Coat the parsnip with olive oil and curry powder and fry until golden brown.

Bombay Potatoes
2 cold boiled potatoes (cubed)   1 small onion (sliced)   1 tomato (chopped)
Tomato juice (left over from the meat curry)   1 teaspoon Madras curry powder

Fry the onion until soft, then add the tomato juice, chopped tomato and curry powder and cook for a few more minutes. Fold in the potato, add a little tomato juice and cook until warmed through.

Mixed Vegetable Curry

Use up all your leftover vegetables in this spicy dish.

1 lb. potatoes (chopped)
9 oz. mixed vegetables (try any combination, as all work well) (chopped small)
1 onion (chopped)   6 cloves of garlic   1 can chopped tomatoes
4 teaspoons curry powder (or to taste)   4 fl. oz. water

Parboil the potatoes for around 10 minutes. Then fry the onion and garlic for a few minutes until soft. Add the curry powder and fry for a further minute, stirring all the time. Add the tomatoes and cook for a further few minutes. Add the vegetables and water, bring to the boil and simmer for 20 minutes until tender. Serve with rice. Serves 4.

"By the Fireside" by Charles Wilson

Bubble and Squeak

*Hot, golden bubble and squeak, served with cold meats
and lashings of homemade chutney.*

1 leek (or onion)
1 lb. mashed potato (even better with a combination of roast potatoes)
**12 oz. cooked vegetables – roast or boiled parsnips, runner beans, Brussels sprouts,
cabbage, carrots, cauliflower, broccoli or peas (all chopped)**
A few cooked chestnuts (optional)
4 rashers of bacon (fried and cut into small strips) or some leftover ham
Salt and black pepper   Oil for frying

Add oil to a frying pan and fry the onions for a few minutes until soft. Add
the bacon or ham and fry until golden. Remove from pan and drain.
Meanwhile, add the mashed potato to a large bowl and fold in the chopped
vegetables, then the onion and bacon and chestnuts (optional). Season with
salt and freshly ground black pepper. Divide the mixture into equal portions
and form into scone-shaped patties. Either fry in the frying pan until golden
both sides, or bake in the oven at 400°F or Mark 6 for 20 to 30 minutes or until
golden. Serve hot with a selection of cold leftover meat (chicken, turkey or
ham ideal) with lashings of homemade chutney. Serves 4 to 6.

Omelette

The easiest leftover recipe for a quick and tasty lunch.

For each omelette:
3 large free-range eggs
A little milk
Selection of fillings
(any leftovers including hard cheese, bacon, vegetables, tomatoes, mushrooms etc)
Seasoning

Beat the eggs together in a bowl and add a little milk and season to taste. Heat oil in frying pan and add filling – cook for a few minutes before adding egg mixture. Place lid on frying pan and cook for around 5 minutes until the egg on the top is not quite set. Slide out onto plate and fold (the internal heat will finish cooking the egg) and serve with a salad and some homemade chutney.

Makes 1 large omelette (use 4 eggs for 2 smaller omelettes).

Savoury Flan

What better way of using up all those tempting savoury titbits in the fridge.

Flan case:
4 oz. margarine   6 oz. flour   2 tablespoons water
Filling:
2 eggs   4 fl. oz. milk   1 onion or leek
Plus a mixture (about a handful) of sliced cooked sausage, ham titbits, cooked bacon scraps, mushrooms, tomatoes, courgettes, broccoli or whatever's in your fridge
Salt and pepper to taste

To make the flan case, place the margarine, flour and 2 tablespoons of water and mix to a firm dough. Roll out on a floured board and line an 8 inch flan tin. Prick the base and bake blind in the oven at 350°F or Mark 4 for 20 minutes or until lightly golden.

Meanwhile, prepare the vegetables. Fry the onions or leeks until soft. Mix the eggs and milk together in a small jug.

Place the onions or leeks in the cooked flan case, top with layers of sliced vegetables and finish with some sliced tomatoes or another colourful vegetable of your choice. Pour over the egg mix, add salt and pepper to taste and bake in the oven at 400°F or Mark 6 for 20 minutes or until set.

Champ

A tasty way of using up those old potatoes and onions.

1 lb. 2 oz. old potatoes   1 large onion or leek
Splash of milk   Knob butter
Black pepper

Boil the potatoes until soft, drain well and mash with a little milk, butter and black pepper. Meanwhile, slice the onion or leek and fry in butter until soft. Fold into the mashed potato. Place potato mixture in an ovenproof dish and bake in preheated oven at 400°F or Mark 6 for 20 minutes or until the topping is crispy and golden. Serve with a warming stew.

Variation – use other cooked leftover vegetables such as 4 oz. grated carrot, broccoli florets, leek, spring onions or mashed swede. Serves 4.

"May Day" by James Hayllar

Bread Pudding

Delicious bread pudding with a sweet pastry crust dusted with cinnamon and sugar.

7 oz. stale bread (broken into small pieces)   8 fl. oz. milk
7 oz. mixed dried fruit (include some chopped cherries)
2 oz. brown sugar   2 teaspoons mixed spice   1 large egg
Cinnamon   Caster sugar
Sweet pastry *(using 7 oz. plain flour, 2 oz. butter, 2 oz. margarine, 1 oz. caster sugar,*
1 egg and a little cold water to mix)

Place bread in a large mixing bowl and pour over the milk and leave for 30 minutes. With a large fork, break and mash the bread mixture until smooth. Add the dried fruit, brown sugar, spice and egg and mix well. Pour into a greased 7 inch square cake tin and smooth over the top.

Make the sweet pastry and roll out and cover the bread pudding, sealing the edges. Bake in preheated oven at 325°F or Mark 3, for an hour or until the pudding is brown. Allow to cool on a wire rack and cut into squares. Dust with cinnamon and caster sugar and serve cold. Makes 6 large portions.

Kedgeree

A favourite breakfast dish.

7 oz. leftover cooked cold fish (any)
3 oz. rice
1 hard boiled egg
Cayenne pepper (small pinch)
Paprika (for decoration)
Large knob butter

Cook the rice in accordance with packet instructions, drain and cool. Meanwhile, flake the fish and chop the hard boiled egg. Melt the butter in a large pan and add the rice, fish, egg and cayenne pepper, mix and heat through until piping hot. Serve on a large platter, with some paprika dusted over the top for a hearty breakfast. Serve 2.

"The Postman Brings News" by Mabel Young

Fish Cakes

Use leftover fish to make them different every time.

8 oz. cooked fish (flaked)
5 oz. cooked potato (mashed)
1 egg yolk   1 egg (beaten)
Handful breadcrumbs
Seasoning   2 tablespoons oil

Heat the oil and add the fish, potatoes, egg yolk and seasoning. Mix well and cook for a few minutes and allow to cool. When cool, form into cakes, brush with the beaten egg and cover with breadcrumbs. Fry the fish cakes until golden brown both sides and serve with a crispy salad.

Alternative – use any leftover fish to add colour and texture to your fish cakes. Add a little grated lemon peel for some extra zing or a few teaspoons of tartar sauce into the mixture before you form the cakes. Makes 4 cakes.

Different proportions of fish and potatoes can be used depending upon the leftovers available.

Fish Salad

A summery, lunchtime salad.

8 oz. cooked fish (roughly flaked)
Salad *(celery, crisp lettuce, cucumber, radish, tomatoes etc)*
1 carrot (grated)   Cress
2 hard boiled eggs
Salad dressing (your favourite)

Cut and prepare the salad items and place in a large bowl. Fold in the flaked fish and hard boiled eggs and then drizzle over your favourite salad dressing. Sprinkle the salad with grated carrot and some cress for colour and serve with crusty bread for a delicious summer lunch.

Fruit Crumble

There's never a better opportunity of using up a selection of fruits to make this tangy crumble – and it's different everytime.

For the filling:
1½ lb. fruit *(try any tasty combination – apples, rhubarb, blackberries, plums etc)*
4 oz. demerara sugar

For the crumble topping:
7 oz. combination of flour and leftover muesli
4 oz. margarine   4 oz. demerara sugar
Lemon juice (one lemon)   Rolled oats (handful)

Prepare your selection of fruit (peel, core, stone etc) and slice into small pieces. Place in saucepan with the lemon juice and sugar and simmer gently for 10 minutes. Meanwhile, make the crumble by placing the flour, margarine and sugar in a bowl and, using your fingers or a processor, mix to a breadcrumb consistency. Place the stewed fruit into an ovenproof dish and top with the crumble mix. Sprinkle a handful of rolled oats over the top and bake in a pre-heated oven at 400°F or Mark 6 for 30 minutes. Serve with leftover cold custard, cream or a dollop of ice cream from the freezer.

Breakfast Muffins

A tasty breakfast-time treat using leftover greens.

2 oz. cooked green vegetables *(leeks, broccoli, or sprouts ideal)*
5 oz. self-raising flour   1 oz. grated cheese
3 fl. oz. milk   ½ teaspoon mustard
1 tablespoon olive oil   1 small egg
Black pepper

Mash the vegetables well and mix with the flour and half the grated cheese. In a separate bowl, whish the milk, egg, mustard and olive oil together and then fold into the vegetables and flour mixture, stirring well. Season with black pepper. Divide between 6 greased muffin moulds and sprinkle with the remaining cheese, then bake in a preheated oven at 400°F or Mark 6 for 25 minutes or until cooked. Serve for breakfast with bacon and a poached egg.

"The Straw Plaiting School" by George Brownlow

Banana Bread

Here's a delicious cake using those remaining bananas
lurking at the bottom of the fruit bowl.

8 oz. self-raising flour
3 oz. butter or margarine
6 oz. demerara sugar
2 free-range eggs
1 lb. bananas (peeled weight)
3 oz. walnuts

Cream the butter and sugar and then add the eggs, a little at the time, together with the sifted flour. Mash the bananas, chop the walnuts and fold into the cake mix. Place in a lined bread tin and bake in a preheated oven at 350°F or Mark 4 for 1 to 1¼ hours.

Variation – use 4 oz. grated carrot and a pinch of allspice instead of the bananas.

Tea Bread

We all have cold tea left over, so here's a way to use it up.

1 cup cold tea
1 cup sultanas
1 cup all bran
1 cup brown sugar
1 cup self-raising flour
1 egg (beaten)

Simply soak the fruit and sugar in the cold tea over night in the fridge. In the morning, add the all bran, flour and the egg and mix well. Place in a small greased or lined loaf tin and bake in a cool oven at 325°F or Mark 3 for 1½ hours until cooked.

Serve with your next afternoon cup of tea.

"First Steps" by Carlton Smith

Homemade Chutney

Delicious, tangy chutney made from leftover fruits and vegetables.

**Use this as your guideline recipe –
depending on what fruit or vegetables you have left over:
1 lb. selection of marrow, pumpkin or courgette
1 lb. tomatoes** *(overripe ones from your greenhouse surplus)*
**1 lb. apples (old bruised ones in the fruit bowl are ideal)
5 oz. onions or leeks   6 fl. oz. white wine vinegar
3 fl. oz. water
Pickling spice bag** *(or make your own with a few of each – dried chilli flakes, ginger,
cloves, black peppercorns, coriander seeds and mustard seeds)*
Pinch sea salt

Use a large heavy saucepan. Place all the ingredients into the pan, together with the spice bag. Over a low heat, simmer gently for 1 hour, stirring regularly. Add a little more water if the chutney dries out. The chutney is cooked when reduced to a thick and rich consistency and you can see the base of the pan when dragging your wooden spoon through it. Spoon into sterilised jars and seal with plastic coated lid. Leave to mature (if you can!) for a few weeks before eating.

Tomato Soup

*If you grow your own tomatoes, then this is a wonderful way
of using up your surplus crop.*

**1 lb. fresh tomatoes (skinned in boiling water and chopped)
1 large onion (chopped)   1 stick celery (sliced)
1 carrot (diced)   1 quart vegetable stock
1 teaspoon sugar   Seasoning to taste
Basil leaves to decorate   Olive oil for frying**

Fry the onion, carrot and celery in the oil for a few minutes, then cover and cook for a further 10 minutes until soft. Add the sugar, seasoning and tomatoes and cook for 5 minutes, stirring well. Then add the stock, bring to the boil and simmer for 15 minutes. Allow to cool, then whiz with a blender until smooth. Reheat and serve with basil leaves floating on the soup.

Potato and Vegetable Soup

A delicious and filling soup to use up all those leftover vegetables.

4 medium potatoes   1 onion or leek (or both)
1 lb. raw vegetables *(use any selection from what you have in the vegetable rack)*
Vegetable stock cube   Half cup rolled oats
Freshly ground black pepper   Water to cover

In a large saucepan, fry the onion or leek until soft. Roughly chop the potatoes and vegetables and add to the pan, together with the crumbled stock cube, black pepper and oats. Pour over sufficient water to just cover the vegetables and simmer for 30 minutes until tender. Remove from the heat and allow to cool slightly, then whiz with hand blender until creamy. Serve hot with a chunk of crusty bread or cool, place in fridge, and reheat the following day.

Serves 4 but you can easily make more or less.

Variation – if you have any cooked vegetables left over, then make the soup as above, but add and simmer the cooked vegetables for the final 10 minutes. Also, if you have a small amount of ham or cooked bacon left over, add after you have blended the soup.

Yesterday's-dinner Soup

Recipe uses one leftover cooked dinner, which makes a delicious lunchtime soup for two.

1 portion cooked potato (mashed, boiled, roast or jacket)
1 portion cooked vegetables (any selection)
1 portion meat (chicken, beef, turkey, lamb)
1 portion gravy plus a little water if required
1 portion sauce – mustard or cranberry or mint or horseradish – depending on meat
Salt and pepper to taste

Place all the ingredients in the blender and blend, adding a little water as required. Season according to taste and heat in a saucepan until hot. Serve in a mug with some crusty bread.

"Washing Day" by Pierre Frère

"Whatever" Salad

Create delicious salads from a variety of leftover goodies.

Lettuce
Selection of salads
(onion, tomatoes, cucumber, jalapeno peppers, broccoli (blanched and cooled),
bean sprouts, mushrooms, etc)
Selection of fruit *(1 apple, orange or lime work best)*
Handful of nuts
(use whatever is available in your cupboard – walnuts and peanuts work best)
Salad dressing of your choice

Line a salad bowl with the lettuce leaves. Prepare the selection of vegetables by washing and slicing and mix with a little of the salad dressing. Peel and slice the fruit and layer over the top of the salad. Sprinkle over the chopped nuts and serve immediately with leftover cold meat and pickles.

Fresh Tomato Soup

Ideal for your favourite pasta dishes.

1 lb. fresh tomatoes (skinned in boiling water and chopped)
1 onion (chopped)
2 cloves garlic (crushed)
1 tbsp tomato purée
Salt and freshly ground black pepper
Sprig of fresh basil (chopped)
2 tbsp olive oil

Fry the onion and garlic in the oil until soft, then add the tomatoes, basil and tomato purée, season and simmer for a further 15 minutes until the sauce thickens. Serve with cooked pasta. Serves 4.

"A Calm Sea" by William Midwood

Fruit Comport

A delicious tangy comport with so many tasty uses.

2 medium eating apples (peeled, cored, chopped)
8 oz. rhubarb (sliced)
3 fl. oz. orange juice
A pinch of cinnamon

Place the apples, rhubarb, orange juice and cinnamon into a heavy-based pan and cook over a low heat for about 15 minutes or until just tender. Serve warm with pancakes, ice cream or rice pudding.

Vegetable Wedges

Create a tasty and colourful platter of chips.

Selection of potatoes, carrots, parsnips (one of each will serve 2)
1 clove of garlic
Olive oil

Cut your selection of vegetables into wedges (leaving skin on) and parboil for 10 minutes. Drain well and pat dry with kitchen towel. In the meantime, heat the olive oil in a baking tray in a hot oven at 425°F or Mark 7 and carefully ladle in the vegetables and crushed garlic. Bake for 30 to 40 minutes until crisp and golden.

Leftover Jam

Nothing beats homemade jam for teatime.

10 oz. leftover fruit *(select strawberries, raspberries, blackberries or a mixture of all)*
10 oz. caster sugar

Place the fruit in a large heavy-bottomed pan with the caster sugar and crush lightly with the back of a spoon. Bring gently to the boil and remove any scum that comes to the surface. Boil for around 5 to 10 minutes to reduce the jam until thick and 'ploppy'. Pour into a bowl and allow to cool. Keep in fridge and use within a few days – if it lasts that long!

Serve with crusty bread, dolloped on rice pudding or with some warm homemade scones.

METRIC CONVERSIONS

The weights, measures and oven temperatures used in the preceding recipes can be easily converted to their metric equivalents. The conversions listed below are only approximate, having been rounded up or down as may be appropriate.

Weights

Avoirdupois	Metric
1 oz.	just under 30 grams
4 oz. (¼ lb.)	app. 115 grams
8 oz. (½ lb.)	app. 230 grams
1 lb.	454 grams

Liquid Measures

Imperial	Metric
1 tablespoon (liquid only)	20 millilitres
1 fl. oz.	app. 30 millilitres
1 gill (¼ pt.)	app. 145 millilitres
½ pt.	app. 285 millilitres
1 pt.	app. 570 millilitres
1 qt.	app. 1.140 litres

Oven Temperatures

	°Fahrenheit	Gas Mark	°Celsius
Slow	300	2	150
	325	3	170
Moderate	350	4	180
	375	5	190
	400	6	200
Hot	425	7	220
	450	8	230
	475	9	240

Flour as specified in these recipes refers to plain flour unless otherwise described.